— ADVENTURES

Don't take photos, make photos!

Jan von Holleben

Text by
Monte Packham

Thames & Hudson

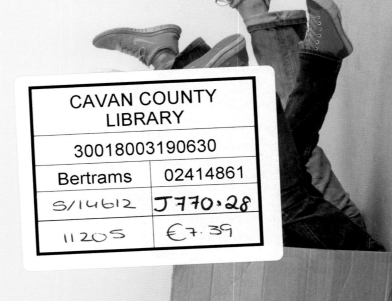

WHAT'S INSIDE?

8   **Everybody Say Cheese!**

10   **Let the Games Begin!**

12   **Flying Dreams**

20   **Brain X-rays**

28   **Fear of Falling**

36   **Faraway Lands**

44   **Fashion Show**

52   **Balancing Game**

58   **Hide and Seek**

66   **Wild Things**

74   **Magic Machines**

80   **Mirror Monsters**

88   **Handy Hints**

92   **Photo School**

EVERYBODY

I'm Jan von Holleben and I'm
a professional photographer.
This bouncy book shows you
loads of wonderful tricks I use
to make photography a game.
Are you ready to play?!

SAY CHEESE!

Photography isn't just about taking photos. It's about transforming the world around you into something fun and magical where anything is possible – where you can fly, become your favourite superhero, twist your limbs like spaghetti, lick your way through a lolly landscape, and much much more…

LET THE GAMES

To start playing you will need:

- A camera (any kind will do – smartphone or digital)

- Friends and family to be your photo models, assistants and playmates

- A good eye and steady hand

- Crazy costumes, treasures and trinkets, and bits and bobs to create your new characters and surroundings

- An endless imagination!

Be Safe
The activities in this book are designed for children 7 years or older. When the book recommends that you ask for help from an adult, make sure you do! Taking photographs from a height, handling mirrors and standing on ladders are all activities that could be dangerous if you don't have the right help.

BEGIN!

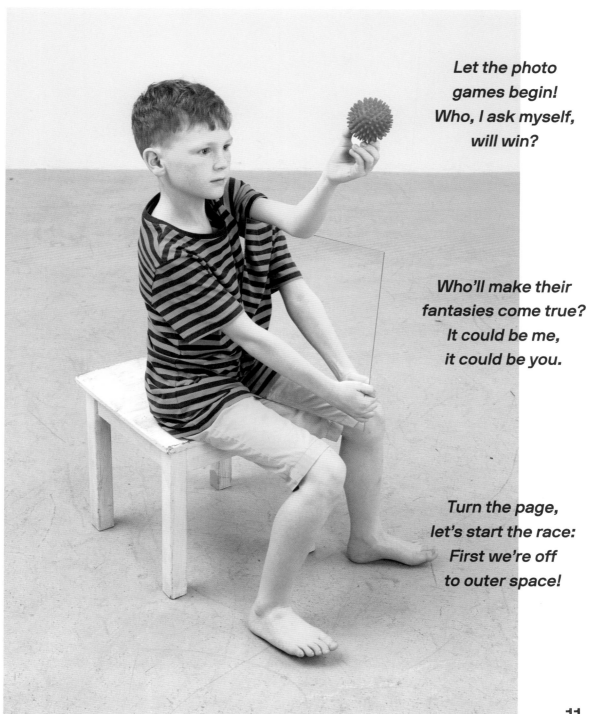

Let the photo
games begin!
Who, I ask myself,
will win?

Who'll make their
fantasies come true?
It could be me,
it could be you.

Turn the page,
let's start the race:
First we're off
to outer space!

FLYING

DREAMS

Angels fly and rockets too;
With photo tricks now so can you!

What are your flying dreams?
To whiz through the air like a
trapeze artist?

To swing through the jungle like Tarzan?
To flap your stingray wings in a tropical ocean?
Or just to let the wind carry you up, up and away?

HOW TO
REACH NEW HEIGHTS

YOU WILL NEED:

- A ladder or adult with strong shoulders

- An empty school playground or backyard

- Flying-themed props

1. First grab some zippy props and costumes to get your ideas off the ground. *Capes and wings, those zingy things? A witch's broom on which to zoom? Propeller hat? Just fancy that!*

2. To take your photo you have to get up high. A ladder, balcony, giraffe's neck or your parent's shoulders will do. Just make sure there's a grown-up to hold you tight.

3. Looking down you can now arrange your photo as you please. Ask your models to lie down and pose like they're flying through the air. The ground's become the sky and the sky's the limit!

1

2

3

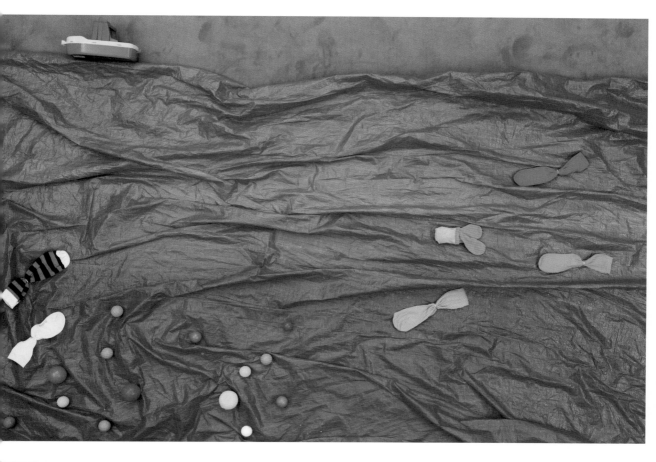

BRAIN

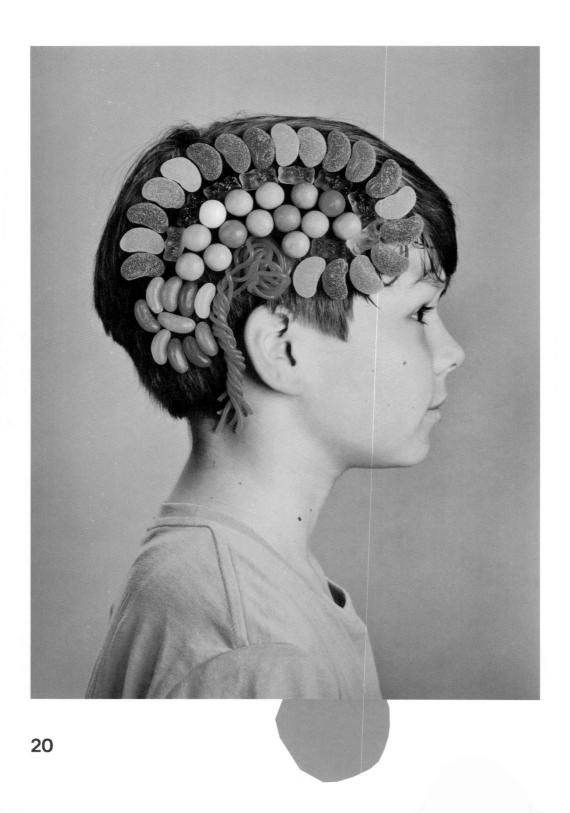

Hey there all you photo maniacs!
Time to morph into photo brainiacs!

**What secrets are you hiding in that
head of yours?**

**Are you a bright spark full of smart
ideas to change the world?
Or is the world just one planet
in your private universe?**

*Your magic thoughts will flash gold, pink
And blue before you know it.
Go stroke your beard (it helps one think) –
But first you need to grow it!*

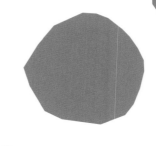

HOW TO
EXPAND YOUR BRAIN

YOU WILL NEED:

- A printed photo of yourself

- A flat surface like a table or the floor

- Objects that sum up your thoughts

- Long arms or a selfie stick

1. Get a photoprint of yourself (or a friend) – the bigger the better and best with a plain background. Brainstorm! Collect all the objects that reveal your invisible selves.

2. Arrange the collage objects on top of your photo (no need to stick them down).

3. When you're happy, photograph your collage.

4. Ta-da! Your extra-straw-dinary portrait is ready to go.

3

4

FEAR OF

FALLING

Photos change your fear of falling
Into your creative calling!

Falling used to really scare me,
Now I love it – go on, dare me!
I soar and glide, I plunge and swoop,
Like airplanes I do loop the loop!

HOW TO
TURN PHOTOGRAPHY ON ITS HEAD

1. Find an empty corner in a room with a bare floor and walls. Bend, twist and fold yourself into your falling pose.

2. Have your photo taken, then turn it on its side.

3. Abracadabra! Left and right become up and down, and you're tumbling through space.

YOU WILL NEED:

- An empty corner with plenty of space around it

- Flexible assistants

1

2

FARAWAY

Pack your bags for far-off lands –
Where we go is in your hands!

Mighty stalks throughout Wheat City
Touch the clouds so light and pretty.

Flower Town has huge hydrangeas
Blooming bright without a danger.

A sandy desert, snowy hills?
They're both exotic, full of thrills.
Go make your own in which to play,
I'll meet you there – so what d'ya say?

YOU WILL NEED:

- Flat ground in a backyard or park

- A sturdy bench

- Objects to build your world with

- Props for your explorers

HOW TO
CHANGE YOUR PERSPECTIVE

1. To begin your journey, construct your fantasy landscape up close to the camera. Lie low to the ground and if you can adjust the aperture on your camera, set it between 11 and 22 so everything is sharp and in focus.

2. Behind this (and a little higher up), should be a place where your friends can climb and explore your new reality. A bench is perfect.

3. As your landscape is nearer to the camera than your friends, you'll find they have suddenly arrived in a mega world where cool distortions fool proportions!

1

2

3

FASHION

SHOW

Start to rule the world of fashion
With your newfound photo passion!

Try a headdress lush and green,
Fitting for a pixie queen.

Or is your fancy fashion look
Just based upon a good old book?

Why not choose a cool disguise,
Like stacks of shades that cause surprise?

HOW TO
FASHION A COMPLETELY NEW LOOK

YOU WILL NEED:

- A mirror without a frame like on a bathroom cupboard

- Some trendy friends

- Interesting objects from around the house

1. Ask your model to hold a mirror in the centre of their face. Get other friends to position your fashion props (pencils, flippers, Grandma's slippers?) so they stick out on one side and are reflected in the mirror.

2. Make sure you can't see your assistants' hands holding the objects, and that your model's headdress is as wacky as possible. Then lights, camera, action – snap your friend's new do!

Don't tell them what their look will be,
Don't let them ever know it –
Until your photo's there to see
And you decide to show it.

1

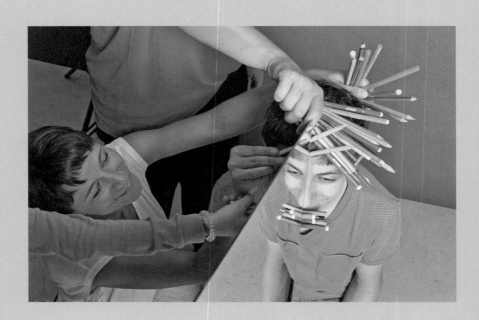

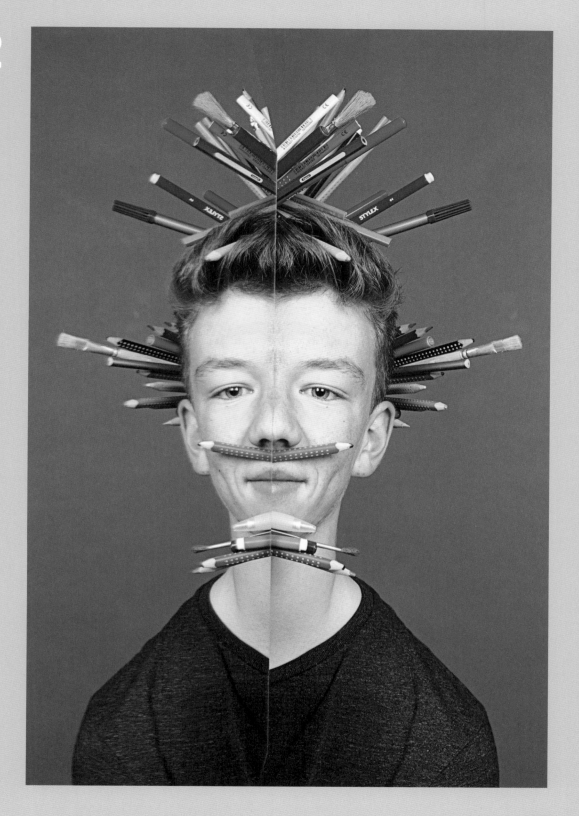

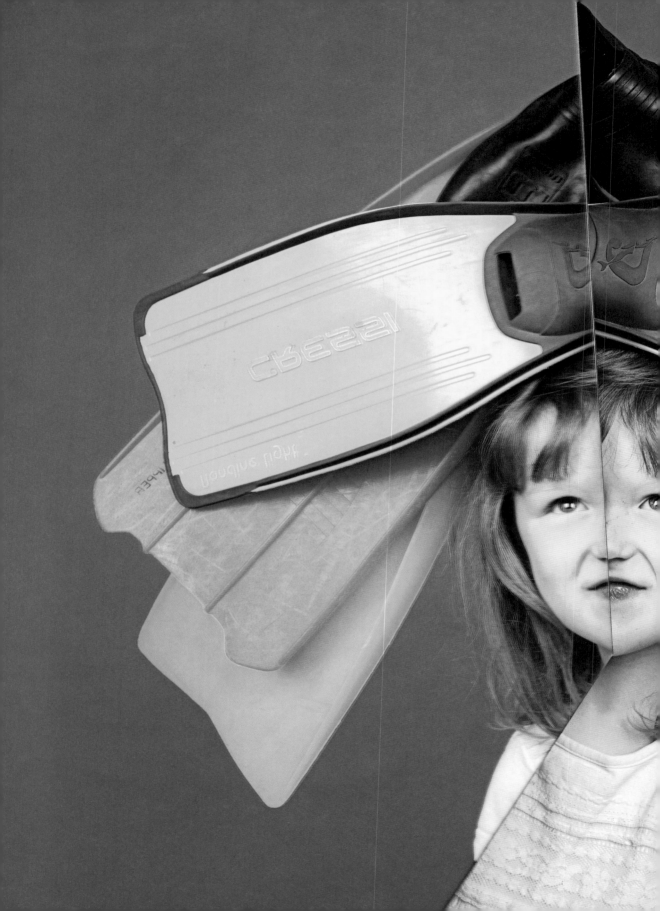

BALANCING

Wibbly wobbly is this game,
Tipsy topsy, never tame!

YOU WILL NEED:

- A large room
  or backyard

- Mixed objects
  of all sizes

- A tripod or low
  table to rest
  your camera on

1. Clear a big space on the floor and wall
   behind. Arrange your objects across the
   floor, so from the angle of the camera
   it looks like they're balancing on top of
   one another.

2. Keep your camera nice and low to the
   ground; tilt it slightly downwards. If you
   can change your camera's aperture,
   set it between 11 and 22 to get all in focus.
   Try putting your camera on a tripod or low
   table to keep it perfectly still, and make
   perspective effective!

   They teeter left, they totter right,
   Don't let them topple out of sight!

1

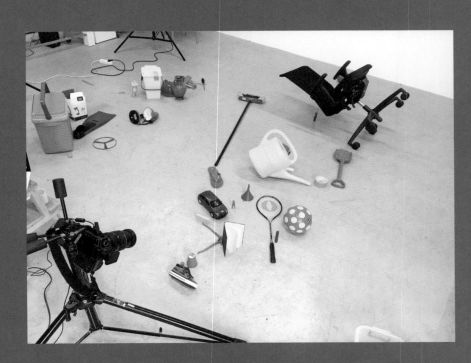

2

HIDE

AND SEEK

A brand-new type of Hide and Seek!
You're curious? Then take a peek...

With mirrors I do clever tricks
That change my legs from two to six.

I conquer gravity and soar
With beating wings right off the floor.

My hand, it likes to creep and crawl
Like spiders up the glassy wall.

At last I all but disappear
And grin five times from ear to ear.

HOW TO
THINK OUTSIDE THE BOX

YOU WILL NEED:

- Cardboard boxes

- Friends who love
  to hide

- Someone to hold the
  box steady outside
  the picture frame

Here's how to play this puzzling game:
Go hide beyond the picture frame!
Then join two photos into one
Like Box Boy here who's having fun.

1. There on the right his head, arms, heart.

2. And on the left? His bottom part!

3. Add left to right: a joined-up shot
   That shows off all the skills you've got.

1

WILD

THINGS

Photography's not for the mild,
But for the daring, brave and wild!

Let's show the world your scary side
With all these creatures as your guide!

One wears a gorgeous gown of shells,
With furry antlers high he yells.

His friends choose corn, pods,
petals, seeds,
To satisfy their monstrous needs.

HOW TO
TAKE A WALK ON THE WILD SIDE

YOU WILL NEED:

- Photos of yourself in freaky poses

- Friends you enjoy foraging with

- A bag to collect nature's bounty

- A board to create your pictures on

1. Take photography on the road! Organise a day trip with your best buddies, perhaps to a: *Jungle, forest, field or plain? Take the sun along – no rain!*

2. Then gather Mother Nature's goodies: *Sticks, bark and berries, Leaves, seeds and cherries; A flower or bud? Some pebbles (no mud)!*

3. Arrange your foraged finds on your fearsome photoprint, laid on the board on the ground. Then rephotograph from above to reveal your wild side.

1

2

3

MAGIC

MACHINES

Invent machines that squeak and pop,
Don't let your factory ever stop!

HOW TO
MANUFACTURE MAGIC

YOU WILL NEED:

- A large surface

- Objects including all kinds of balls: bouncy balls, ping pong balls, golf balls, space balls…

- Blu Tack to hold things in place

1. Clear some space on a table or a mat (away from pets and little people who like grabbing things).

2. Raid the recycling bin, garage and toy box for machine parts.

3. Use your go-go-gadget arms or selfie stick to photograph your machine from above.

*Collect odd balls, wheels and old bottles –
Transform them into lights, cogs, throttles!*

1

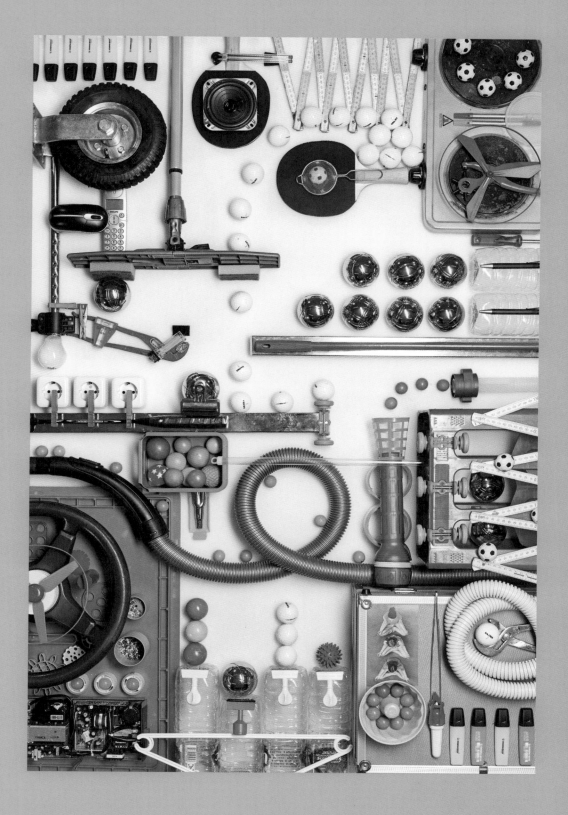

MIRROR

MONSTERS

Mirror monsters! Creepy creatures,
Crazy critters with friends' features!

Reflect upon these ghoulish guys
Who gawp and gape with glaring eyes!

With doubled arms and doubled palms
They hypnotise with kooky charms.

With four strong legs or bent ones small
They stand up tall or float – don't fall!

HOW TO
BEFRIEND MONSTERS

YOU WILL NEED:

- A full-length mirror, like on a wardrobe door

- Friends who know each other well

- Coloured clothing

1. To bring your own monsters to life, find yourself a tall mirror that goes all the way to the floor.

2. Place your friend half behind the mirror and let it complete your picture.

Adjust its limbs left, right, up, down,
Until your monster smiles its frown!

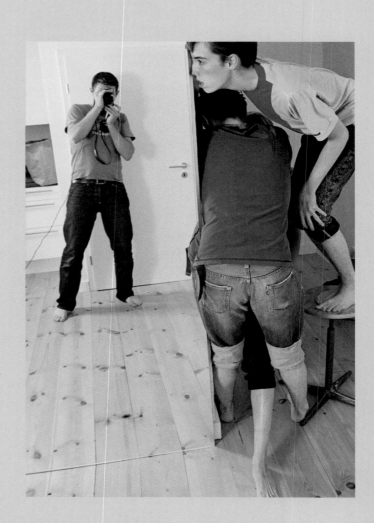

HANDY

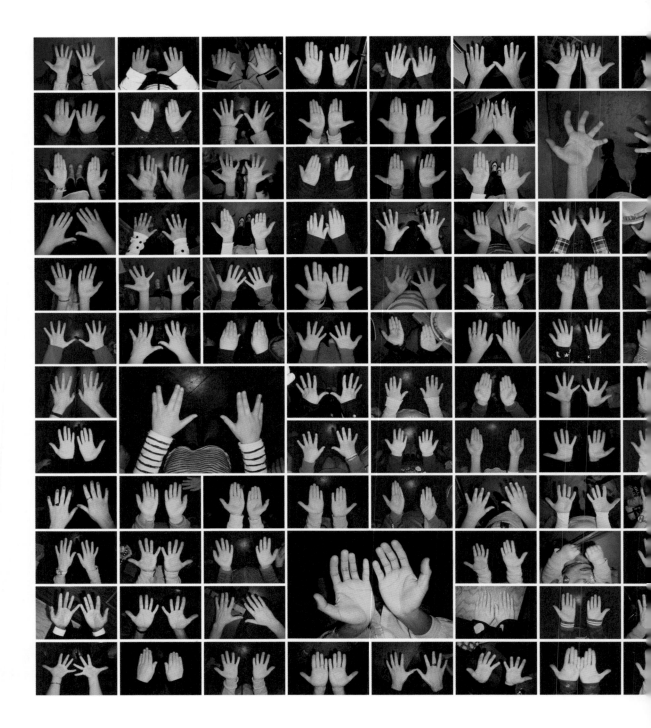

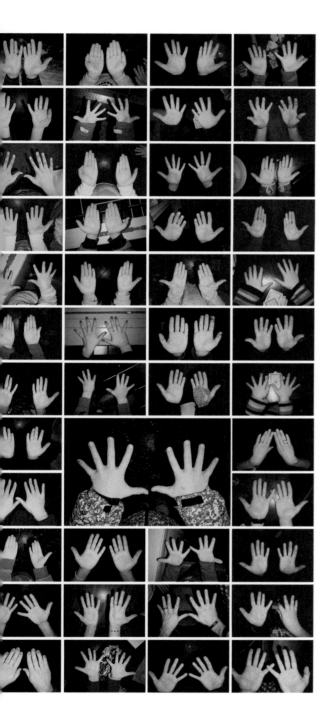

You're nearly there, you photo star;
These tip-top tips will take you far!

Now that you've enjoyed all the adventures in this book, it's time to head off on some of your own. But just before you do, here are some secret tips to help you on your way...

COLOUR

*Colour's not just what it seems
But how we see it in our dreams!
So red's not red but strawberry pies
And green is gleaming python eyes,
While yellow is like mermaids' hair
And blue is sapphires, bright and rare.*

JUXTAPOSITION

*Just juxtapose – go mix things up!
A fruit'n'veggie ice cream cup!
You turn the world upon its head
When opposites attract instead.
Like young and old, big and small,
Shy and bold, or short and tall.*

COMPOSITION
What goes where?
Up, down, here, there,
Left, right, or in the middle?
Frame and balance,
Place with care
To solve each photo riddle.

YOU'RE IN CHARGE
Photographers choose what to do:
Who, where to shoot,
Which dreams come true.
Enjoy arranging everyone
But don't be bossy, keep it fun.

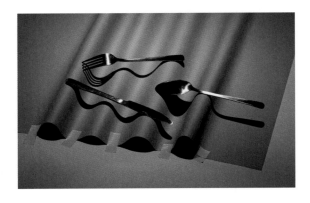

LIGHT
When used together dark and light
Create bold patterns stark and bright.
The best conditions? Cloudy days
With mellow sun, no harsh rays.

PHOTO

SCHOOL

The more you learn,
The more you'll know
To make your photos
Grow and grow!

No doubt you'll go on your photo adventures with a spiffy smartphone in your hands. But if you'd like to use a professional camera some day, here are some brainy things to keep in mind.

APERTURE

Aperture is the tiny hole in your camera lens that lets light into the camera. It also controls the depth of field, or how much of your photo is in focus. A large aperture lets in more light but less of your photo will be in focus. A small aperture lets in less light but more of your photo will be in focus.

SHUTTER SPEED

The shutter's the little door that opens and shuts to let light into your camera. How long to keep it open? Fast shutter speeds freeze action, like individual raindrops. Slow shutter speeds blur moving things, like a tumbling waterfall.

FOCAL LENGTH

Make focal length your photo strength!
Focal length lets you choose how much of a view you capture in your picture and how big things appear in it.

FOCUS

Hocus-pocus, keep in focus!
In-focus things are crisp and sharp. Out-of-focus things are soft and fuzzy. Use focus to highlight what's really important in your photos.

LENSES

Bim bam boom, it's time to zoom!
A zoom lens brings you up close to teeny-weeny
objects and makes faraway sights seem really near.
A wide-angle lens gives you googly fish eyes,
so you can see aaaall the way from left to right.

CROPPING

There's nothing hard in photo cropping,
It's no more than photo chopping!
What are the boundaries of your photo?
What to include and what to cut out?
Sometimes showing less is showing more.

PHOTOPRINTS

How will you make your photoprints?
There's many kinds, so here's some hints.
All loud and glossy, colours bright?
Or quiet and matt in black and white?
It doesn't matter; big or small,
Just hang them proudly on your wall!

A very, very big THANK YOU goes to all my little and big friends, their friends, their friends' friends, as well as to their parents, grandparents, siblings, uncles, aunts and guardians who contributed to this book. Without their great sense of humour, excitement, playfulness and trust in my work as photographer, this book and all its images would not have been possible. This book is for you and for all our new friends in the future who also love to play with photography.

Jan von Holleben

Be Safe
The activities suggested in this book should not be completed without adult supervision. To the extent permitted by law, no liability is accepted by the Author, the Photographer or Thames & Hudson for any loss, damage or injury arising as a consequence of attempting the activities described in this book.

First published in the United Kingdom in 2019 by Thames & Hudson Ltd, 181A High Holborn, London WC1V 7QX

Photo Adventures © 2019 Thames & Hudson Ltd, London
Photographs by Jan von Holleben © 2019 Jan von Holleben
Text by Monte Packham © 2019 Thames & Hudson Ltd, London

British Library Cataloguing-in-Publication Data
A catalogue record for this book is available from the British Library

ISBN 978-0-500-65157-5

Printed and bound in China by Everbest Printing Co. Ltd

To find out about all our publications, please visit **www.thamesandhudson.com**. There you can subscribe to our e-newsletter, browse or download our current catalogue, and buy any titles that are in print.